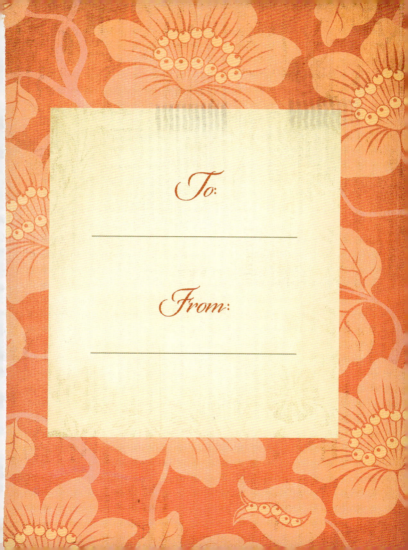

To:

_____

From:

_____

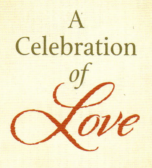

A
Celebration
of
Love

A HELEN STEINER RICE® PRODUCT

ISBN 978-1-61626-609-7

Devotional writing provided by Nanette Anderson, Rebecca Currington, and Elece Hollis in association with Snapdragon Groupsm Tulsa, OK.

Cover and interior design: Greg Jackson, Thinkpen Graphic Design

Published by Barbour Publishing, Inc., P.O. Box 719, Uhrichsville, Ohio 44683 www.barbourbooks.com

Our mission is to publish and distribute inspirational products offering exceptional value and biblical encouragement to the masses.

ecpa Member of the Evangelical Christian Publishers Association

Printed in India.

A
Celebration
of
Love

A Keepsake Devotional Featuring the
Inspirational Poetry of Helen Steiner Rice

BARBOUR

CONTENTS

INTRODUCTION

Celebrating Love

Love is the gold filament that overlays all of life from our relationships to our actions and behaviors, thoughts and perceptions. It is the force that counters loneliness and despair, pain and suffering, grief and heartache. It is the engaging ingredient that draws out the best in us, gives us a song in the night, and causes us to see the good in others. Love is the remedy for life's difficulties and the reward for life's goodness. It is the essence of God.

As you read through the pages of this book, we pray you will be blessed and inspired by the beautiful and insightful poetry of Helen Steiner Rice. Each poem has been coupled with a devotional thought to enhance her message to give love first place in your marriage, your family, your friendships, and your relationship with God. It is your highest calling, what you were born to do, and follows the example set by your heavenly Father.

God bless you as we celebrate love together.

The Magic *of* Love

Love is like magic and it always will be,
For love still remains life's sweet mystery.
Love works in ways that are wondrous and strange,
And there's nothing in life that love cannot change.
Love can transform the most commonplace
Into beauty and splendor and sweetness and grace.
Love is unselfish, understanding, and kind,
For it sees with its heart and not with its mind.
Love gives and forgives; there is nothing too much
For love to heal with its magic touch.
Love is the language that every heart speaks,
For love is the one thing that every heart seeks. . .
And where there is love God, too, will abide
And bless the family residing inside.

~HSR

Celebrating
Love's Meaning
and Purpose

The Gift *of a* Lasting Love

Love is much more than a tender caress
And more than bright hours of happiness,
For a lasting love is made up of sharing
Both hours that are joyous and also despairing.
It's made up of patience and deep understanding
And never of stubborn or selfish demanding.
It's made up of climbing the steep hills together
And facing with courage life's stormiest weather.
And nothing on earth or in heaven can part
A love that has grown to be part of the heart.
And just like the sun and the stars and the sea,
This love will go on through eternity. . . .

~HSR

A Love That Thrives

*For this reason a man will leave his father and mother
and be united to his wife, and they will become one flesh.*

GENESIS 2:24 NIV

L ove, in all its stages, is very much like a tree. Its romantic beginnings are small, tender, easily bruised and broken. Its delicate roots thrive on the simple nourishment of a first exciting kiss and tentative embrace.

The decision to open the earth together and put the roots of promise into the ground of marriage is often fraught with questions: Will the soil be rich enough to nurture it? Are its supports strong enough to keep it standing in any wind? Is it exposed to enough sun, enough moisture? Are we committed to fertilizing it regularly?

Lasting love is a constantly growing creation that must be carefully tended. It needs gentleness in the planting and the good support of family and friends to help it weather the inevitable storms that will come. It must have the nurturing sunlight of selflessness, empathy, and encouragement, and roots ever seeking the deep Living Water of God's wisdom and instruction. It must be resilient enough to bear with patience the painful pruning that produces a strong, straight trunk.

A neglected tree will falter, weaken, and die; but with proper care it will—like a healthy love—sprout sturdy, gracious branches of protection, sparkling joy, and a rich beauty that bless all who look upon it!

WHAT IS LOVE?

What is love? No words can define it—
It's something so great only God could design it.
Wonder of wonders, beyond man's conception—
And only in God can love find true perfection. . .
And love can transform the most commonplace
Into beauty and splendor and sweetness and grace. . .
For love is unselfish, giving more than it takes—
And no matter what happens love never forsakes.
It's faithful and trusting and always believing,
Guileless and honest and never deceiving.
Yes, love is beyond what man can define,
For love is immortal and God's gift is divine!

~HSR

Love's True Meaning

*This is love: not that we loved God, but that he loved us
and sent his Son as an atoning sacrifice for our sins.*

1 JOHN 4:10 NIV

If we were to put all the world's languages together, there would be literally dozens of definitions for the word "love." In every culture known to us, love is used to express everything from lust to our favorite foods! It has been packaged up with crushes, illicit affairs, casual cravings, and enchantment with material things.

But real love is something quite different from all this! The Bible uses the word love to describe how God feels about us and how those loving feelings caused Him to take action. God's first love gift to us was the creation of a world so vast, filled with such variety and beauty and mind-boggling detail, that we cannot fully comprehend it—a gift that blesses us daily!

The wonder of God's love through nature, however, can never come close to the love He expressed in sending His only

Son—not only to save our lives but to give us abundant life when we had no way to gain it on our own.

God's love is never transient, fickle, casual, or changing. It infuses good marriages, happy families, and lasting friendships. Most importantly, it is the foundation and lifeblood of our relationship with Him. If you have never known it, go to the Source. Your heavenly Father longs to lavish His love on you!

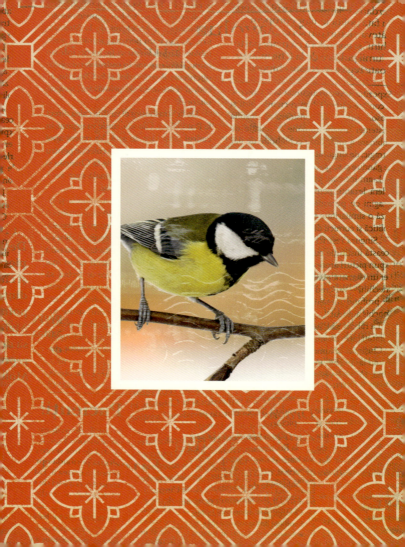

Wings *of* Love

The priceless gift of life is love,
For with the help of God above
Love can change the human race
And make this world a better place. . .
For love dissolves all hate and fear
And makes our vision bright and clear
So we can see and rise above
Our pettiness on wings of love.

~HSR

Be Free!

*The Lord is the Spirit, and where
the Spirit of the Lord is, there is liberty.*

2 CORINTHIANS 3:17 NASB

L ove is meant to take flight! Have you ever noticed how often love is symbolized by things that rise and soar: a bird's wings, a waving banner, the heights of ecstasy, sitting on top of the world?

To be loved is to be raised up out of the mundane, the ordinary, the baseness of our lives. The Bible says that even when we were unlovely God loved us, coming to earth in human form to lift us out of the sin that drags us low, makes us dirty, ashamed, and convinced there is no hope.

Perfect love transforms. . .overwhelming hate, overcoming despair, able to lift a darkened heart bound by loathing, defeat, and fear so it can soar like a feather skipping across the blue dome of the sky.

To grasp that God loves us is freedom from the chains of all those dark and ugly things that would hold us down.

Ask Him to remove your fetters and let you rise to the joy of His perfect love. To receive it is to be lifted above hate and fear and anger, to share it with another is to send it fluttering above earthly things to bless and comfort and heal our world.

REMEMBER THIS

Great is the power of might and mind,
But only love can make us kind,
And all we are or hope to be
Is empty pride and vanity.
If love is not a part of all,
The greatest man is very small.

~HSR

What We Really Need

This is how God showed his love among us: He sent his one and only Son into the world that we might live through him.

1 JOHN 4:9 NIV

Most of us know all too well the life stories of famous men, titans in their fields, driven from a very early age to achieve, to amass great wealth and notoriety. When asked, "How much money is enough?" one such multi-millionaire replied, "Just a little more!"

Why is this so? Why aren't money, power, and prestige enough to make us happy? What is that "little more" we're seeking?

The missing link is love! Without it, everything we attempt will eventually ring false, leave us flat and unfulfilled. Biographies abound of men and women whose greed and avarice were simply a mask for the hunger to be loved, to be cherished not for what they'd done, but for who they were.

The Bible teaches that each and every one of us is precious and loved by God. Do you doubt it? Are you trusting vain and empty worldly accomplishments because you think they will somehow make you more worthy of approval by God and men?

It is a futile exercise. Trust only God's transforming mercies to infuse your efforts with value greater than the world can measure. Bathe every thought, deed, and motive in the light of His love and grace. It will change you—and you, no matter how great or small your achievements, might just change the world!

Another Link *of* Love

It takes a special day like this
To just look back and reminisce
And think of things you've shared together
Through sunny, fair, and stormy weather,
And how both smiles as well as tears
Endear true love across the years. . .
For there is no explaining of
The mystery of the bond of love,
Which just grows richer, deeper, stronger
Because you've shared it one year longer.

~HSR

Times to Remember

I thank my God in all my remembrance of you.

PHILIPPIANS 1:3 NASB

Scientists gauge our planet's age or the time of certain geologic events by drilling through the earth's crust and counting the layers of sediment. Each one represents a period in our history. With intensive study, we often get a surprisingly clear picture of events as they unfolded through eons. Important work, because it helps us to see things we've done right and actions that went astray.

In much the same way, the years of marriage continue to stack up, and in their layers is the story of a mingled life—the surprises, the joys, the births and deaths, the mistakes and the victories.

Anniversaries matter and should be celebrated because each year is testament to our growth and unity in faith, to understanding and loving more deeply, to needing and being needed, to remembering the conquered hardships and temptations that have made us stronger.

As your wedding anniversary rolls around this year, take time to honor and celebrate each other and what the two of you have overcome and accomplished together. Dig down to the very bottom of your memory box. Laugh, cry, examine each layer of life; be amazed at what God has done as a beautiful result of the two of you becoming man and wife!

A Pattern *for* Living

"Love one another as I have loved you"
May seem impossible to do,
But if you will try to trust and believe,
Great are the joys that you will receive,
For love makes us patient, understanding, and kind,
And we judge with our hearts and not with our minds,
For as soon as love entered the heart's open door,
The faults we once saw are not there anymore,
And the things that seem wrong begin to look right
When viewed in the softness of love's gentle light. . . .

~HSR

The Fabric of Love

*This is how we know that we love
the children of God: by loving God
and carrying out his commands.*

1 JOHN 5:2 NIV

A good seamstress intent on creating beautiful attire must choose the design, select the fabric, have her sewing machine in good order, and her basket of sewing implements within easy reach. Above all, she must follow the pattern in explicit detail if the end result is to be a well-fitted, beautiful, and durable garment.

The pattern of love that God has traced upon the fabric of our lives is the one He wants us to follow as we love one another. All who have truly experienced God's love can only stand in awe at how wonderfully it is expressed. With what care and attention to detail God has shown His love for our world and the creatures, human and otherwise, that inhabit it.

God's love is unfailing, patient, and kind, full of grace, mercy, and forgiveness. It is selfless, abundant and generous, trusting and faithful, joyful, peaceable, and filled with hope. It always seeks to redeem and re-create.

What an amazing and true pattern! Mastering it is difficult, but with a willing heart and the tools of God's Word and our heavenly Father, the Divine Tailor, standing ever ready to help, we can learn. The result, by His design, will be well-fitted, beautiful, and enduring.

Celebrating

Love, Marriage,

and Romance

ROMANCE

I'd like to be a raindrop
Just falling on your hand,
I'd like to be a blade of grass
On which your dear feet stand,
I'd like to be your shadow
As it moves around all day,
I'd like to be most anything
That hangs around your way.

~HSR

Fan the Flame

Let him kiss me with the kisses of his mouth—
for your love is more delightful than wine.
SONG OF SONGS 1:2 NIV

D
o you remember your first crush? The first time the boy you fancied looked into your eyes with words ears can't hear, the electric joy that rippled through you when finally he held your hand and at long last kissed you gently for the first time?

Ah, romance! There is more poetry written about it than any other subject known to man. So fragile, so fleeting! How easy it is for the busyness and exhaustion of living to crush out the excitement and joy we first felt when we were near the one we love.

Remember this: The more hectic the pace of life, the more we have to rekindle romance. We need the tender touch, the long embrace, the lingering kiss. Even after years and years of marriage, you should cherish sweet reminders that his gaze still melts your heart, that he would not want to live in a world without you.

Love, romantic love, is God's unique gift to us, His human creation. Don't allow neglect or worldly pressures to destroy it. Remember all that made the sweetheart of your youth the love of your life. Travel back to that place of rediscovering, recapturing, and treasuring. Fan the embers of a long-buried passion, and let it burst into flame once more!

Sweetheart

You're lovable, you're wonderful,
You're as sweet as you can be,
There's nobody in all the world
Who means so much to me;
I love you more than life itself,
You make my dreams come true,
Forever is not long enough
For me to be near to you.

~HSR

The Flavors of Life

Taste and see that the LORD is good;
blessed is the man who takes refuge in him.

PSALM 34:8 NIV

Sweetness: The taste on the tongue of fresh water, a ripe peach, a sliver of chocolate, the shivering delight of ice cream!

Sweetly: The way the sensation of joy arises in a victory claimed, a dream revealed, a goal accomplished, a fear mastered. . .answered prayer!

Sweetheart: In all the world, that one and only special love we're all looking for, the one who creates in us a desire and longing no other person or thing on earth can satisfy. The one who makes us laugh and whose absence drives us to tears. The one who looks at us when we're grimy and disheveled and sees only beauty. The one whose opinion matters most, whose words of encouragement lift us up, whose embrace we could not live without.

Here's hoping we all find our sweetheart! And when you do, remember to *be* one, too! Love must never be a 50/50 proposition. It is a 100 percent all-out, no strings attached gift, expending everything for another that characterizes God's love for us. It is selfless, generous, free, and full, exulting in fellowship, rejoicing in forgiveness, desiring to gratify every need, every true hope and prayer and longing.

In a word—SWEET!

HEARTSTRINGS

Pleasant little memories tuggin' at my heart
Keep me thinkin' of you when we are apart,
And with every heart-tug, wishes sweet and true
Leave my heart's door open, and find their way to you,
But I don't mind the tuggin' at my heartstrings
     all year through
Because it's mighty pleasant when it's being done by you.

~HSR

The Tie That Binds

My God shall supply all your need according
to His riches in glory by Christ Jesus.

PHILIPPIANS 4:19 NKJV

How heartrending it is to say good-bye, to take leave through distance or death of our loved ones! Just think how much effort goes into arranging, planning, and spending time with family and friends. And parting never seems to get any easier, no matter how often we must do it.

For two people in love, separation can be the most difficult thing in the world to bear! Love is something to be shared, and when its object is away, we suffer loss and loneliness, and a craving that nothing else can fill.

In creating us, God intended we should enjoy the constant fellowship of His love and friendship. Sin, that great divider, comes between us and our Maker, sending us away from Eden, pitting brother against brother, and setting husband and wife at odds.

God's love is the tie that binds us back to Him and to each other, reconnecting friendships in forgiveness and grace, pulling us together time and again with heartstrings of love to those we long for. Jesus gave His life to heal the rift between sinful man and a righteous God, a rift that can extend into our human relationships as well. Look to Him to heal separation with strong cords of mercy. See with what great longing He waits for you!

May God Bless
Your Wedding Day

May God bless your wedding day
    and every day thereafter
And fill your home with happiness
    and your hearts with love and laughter. . .
And may each year together find you
    more and more in love
And bring you all the happiness
    you're so deserving of.
May the joy of true companionship
    be yours to share through life,
And may you always bless the day
    that made you husband and wife.

~HSR

A Mighty Stream

*Two are better than one, because
they have a good return for their work. . . .
A cord of three strands is not quickly broken.*

ECCLESIASTES 4:9, 12 NIV

Two rivers running separately might meander far apart through differing climates, soils, and views. They rumble through difficult passageways, enjoy expansive freedom, endure harsh treatment, survive pollution, and in some places receive loving care and great respect. They give joy, life, and prosperity, but they are also capable of inflicting great harm. A marriage is like the joining of these rivers, whose very separate and very different flows mingle to create a richer, fuller tide.

God's pure intention for bringing together two lives in marriage is to combine them in a stronger, more comprehensive union. A marriage of hearts is the happy blending of love and experience, laughter and companionship, able to cut through the stubborn rock of hardship and loss, to bubble with pure joy over the stones of bitterness and poverty, running with confidence and faithfulness and combined wisdom into the future tender tributaries of children and friends.

May God bless your wedding day! Know that as you blend your lives into one mighty current, you will need His loving, living water to flow with you, in you, and through you. This is what long-lasting, love-bathed, and successful marriages are made of.

A Prayer *for* the Bride *and* Groom

As hand in hand you enter a life that's bright and new,
May God look down from heaven and bless the two of you.
May He give you understanding, enough to make you kind,
So you may judge each other
    with your hearts and not your minds.
May He teach you to be patient as you learn to live together,
Forgiving little human rifts that arise
    in stormy weather. . .
And may your love be strong enough
    to withstand the strongest sea,
So you may dwell forever in love's rich tranquility.

~HSR

Thundering Waves

[Jesus] got up, rebuked the wind and said
to the waves, "Quiet! Be still!" Then the wind
died down and it was completely calm.

MARK 4:39 NIV

Thomas Moran was famous for his huge and brilliant oil paintings of America's western territories. Some of his lesser known, but no less magnificent paintings, were of ships being tossed on vast thundering ocean waves. He was able to portray the power of the waves and the helplessness of mankind.

Is your love stronger than the waves of trouble and the harshness of life that you might face someday? If God is the stable force of your marriage, your love can grow strong enough to face almost any trial. God's love teaches us to forgive, to forbear, to be kind and understanding. God's love is love stronger than self. It is love that is able when mistreated, not to count the blows or attempt to get revenge. It is the love you need to survive life in wholeness and with peace and joy.

Many days your marriage ship will sail smoothly on calm waters, and tranquility will reign. God is with you in those days. The most wonderful news is that He is there with His people to bless them by still waters when life is sweet, as well as in stormy seas when trouble is upon them. He won't forget you. He won't abandon ship. You can count on Him.

THE MIRACLE *of* MARRIAGE

Marriage is the union of two people in love,
And love is sheer magic, for it's woven of
Gossamer dreams, enchantingly real,
That people in love are privileged to feel. . .
But the exquisite ecstasy that captures the heart
Of two people in love is just a small part
Of the beauty and wonder and miracle of
That growth and fulfillment and evolvement of love. . .
For ecstasy passes, but it is replaced
By something much greater that cannot be defaced,
For what was in part has now become whole,
For on the wings of the flesh, love entered the soul.

~HSR

Old Folks in Love

Above all, keep fervent in your love for one another,
because love covers a multitude of sins.

1 PETER 4:8 NASB

Have you ever watched an elderly couple in a restaurant talking quietly or silent over their dinner? They weren't bubbly and excited about their marriage, it seemed. Did you wonder if they still loved each other?

There's no way to know for sure since every marriage is different. But it might be that they were just quietly enjoying each other's companionship. They may have been so close that they could converse with few words. Their hearts might have been very close and content. This is often the case after years of loving and supporting one another.

The ideas we hold onto about true love tend to make it seem like an almost unattainable miracle, rather than a lifelong adventure. So we judge a couple's marriage prematurely by how it looks from the outside. Yet, the real estimate of a marriage's strength and value can be seen in how the partners face up to troubles and how they relate to each other in the midst of pain, how they support each other, and how they love one another through losses, hurts, and joys.

Love your spouse in a way that matters. Love deep and strong and faithfully. Someday, a young person new to love may see you and think your love has grown stale. You can smile because you know the truth of the matter.

WHAT IS MARRIAGE?

It is sharing and caring,
Giving and forgiving,
Loving and being loved,
Walking hand in hand,
Talking heart to heart,
Seeing through each other's eyes,
Laughing together,
Weeping together,
Praying together,
And always trusting and believing
And thanking God for each other. . .
For love that is shared is a beautiful thing—
It enriches the soul and makes the heart sing.

~HSR

Cookie Swap

Be kind to one another, tenderhearted, forgiving
one another, even as God in Christ forgave you.

EPHESIANS 4:32 NKJV

Ladies in the south like to get together during the holidays for tea and sometimes a cookie swap. You know how it works. Each visitor brings packages of her favorite home-baked cookies. She brings some to sample and share at the tea. Then when she leaves she takes packages of cookies baked by others home with her.

It is much like that in a marriage. There is a lot of give and take. You share, and as you share, you grow. In your marriage there will be times when you will need forgiveness and grace and times when you must give them.

And just like a cookie swap, where there will be batches that taste bad or don't look so fresh, some parts of married life will be hard to take, some pieces you really won't like to accept. Often what you prepared to give won't turn out so well either. Still, you give and take because that's how marriage works.

God is the prime example of giving forgiveness where it is undeserved. He was kind to His enemies and showed grace and acceptance to the outcasts of society.

Two imperfect people living together can't always be in harmony, but with tenderness, kindness, and forgiveness you can have a happy and satisfying marriage.

With God *as* Your Partner

It takes a groom, it takes a bride—
Two people standing side by side.
It takes a ring and vows that say
This is our happy wedding day. . .
And every home is specially blessed
When God is made a daily guest. . .
For married folks who pray together
Are happy folks who stay together,
For when God's love becomes a part
Of body, mind, and soul and heart,
Their love becomes a wondrous blending
That's both eternal and unending—
And God looks down and says, "Well done,"
For now you two are truly one.

~HSR

Look Who's Coming to Dinner

"The virgin will be pregnant. She will have a son, and they will name him Immanuel," which means "God is with us."

MATTHEW 1:23 NCV

At Thanksgiving dinner, a mom set an extra plate and reserved a chair for a mystery guest. She was trying to teach her children to consider Jesus to be an unseen guest at her family's table. Jesus is someone who many families would feel uncomfortable and embarrassed to sit with for a meal. Others would be highly honored by such a visitor. How about you?

Jesus wants to be more than a guest in your home. He wants to live there. Does the invisible, ever-present God go unnoticed and neglected in your home? If you could see Him, would your demeanor and attitude be different? If you allow Him, He will be a guiding presence in your home, holding and molding your family together. He will be a quiet voice of conscience that teaches you to be kind to each other. He will be a comfort in dark times and a light of hope at the end of the tunnel.

In your marriage, give God a place of honor. Set Him a place at the table if you need a reminder that He is near. What strength and grace you will gain if Jesus is recognized there! Remember, *Immanuel* was the name angels called Baby Jesus on the day of His birth. It means "God is with us." And, yes, He is.

WITH FAITH *in* EACH OTHER—
and FAITH *in the* LORD

With faith in each other and faith in the Lord
May your marriage be blessed with love's priceless reward,
For love that endures and makes life worth living
Is built on strong faith and unselfish giving. . .
So have faith, and the Lord will guide both of you through
The glorious new life that is waiting for you.

~HSR

Vital Faith

Faith is the substance of things hoped for,
the evidence of things not seen.

HEBREWS 11:1 NKJV

A tiny boy stood shivering and dripping at the side of the swimming pool. His father stood below him, holding out his big arms saying, "Jump, son. I'll catch you." The boy considered for only a second and then grinned and jumped. Maybe you have seen such a scenario acted out at the pool. If you have, you may have smiled at the faith the boy displayed in his father. Do you have that kind of faith in God and in your spouse?

Faith is an ingredient without which you can't build a good marriage. Faith is trusting and believing in your spouse when things can't be open and controlled. He leaves on a business trip; do you trust him or doubt him? She has the checkbook, do you trust her? He is late again; do you have faith in him? In every relationship there are things that must be accepted on faith.

You will find plenty of opportunities to trust God through the years. You will face some hard things and some difficult situations. You can do it because you can totally trust God to be with you through any valley and as you climb mountains and cross rivers. Obstacles of everyday living are nothing to Him. Joy and contentment can be yours when you learn to trust your spouse and trust the Lord.

WHERE THERE IS LOVE

Where there is love the heart is light,
Where there is love the day is bright.
Where there is love there is a song
To help when things are going wrong.
Where there is love there is a smile
To make all things seem more worthwhile.
Where there is love there's a quiet peace,
A tranquil place where turmoils cease.
Love changes darkness into light
And makes the heart take wingless flight.
Oh, blessed are those who walk in love,
They also walk with God above. . . .

~HSR

Stronger Than the Storm

"The mountains may be removed and the hills may shake,
but My lovingkindness will not be removed from you,
and My covenant of peace will not be shaken."

ISAIAH 54:10 NASB

If you live in a part of the world that is prone to tornados, you may seem a fool to people who live in other regions. Run to a cellar while a tunnel of wind crashes through the sky touching down wherever it may? Ridiculous! If you watch coastal regions where hurricanes are reported, hear news of cyclones, earthquakes, and volcanoes, or see the aftermath of blizzards striking northern cities, or southern lands wrecked by floods, you may think those residents have made a poor choice about where to live.

There are storms wherever you choose to reside. Storms are a part of family life, too. It's a fact we often want to deny. Sickness, death, fire, financial crisis, pain, and loss in other forms may come over the years, and these trials will test the strength of your resolve and of your love itself. Will you love your spouse enough to see him through—enough to brave on through the end of the storm when peace returns?

If you let them, the tough places can be precursors of greater love and appreciation between your spouse and yourself. The giving and selflessness that surviving tribulations require strengthens marriage, making it a haven—a harbor—a refuge where love is bright and hearts are healed.

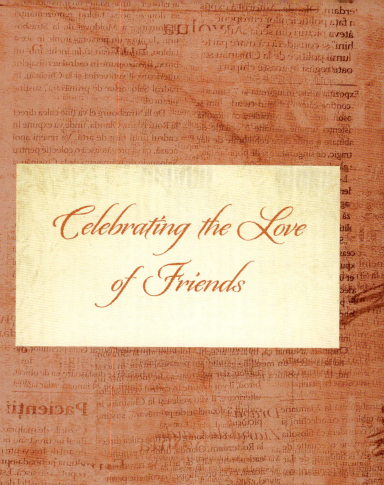

Celebrating the Love of Friends

STRANGERS ARE FRIENDS
WE HAVEN'T MET YET

God knows no strangers, He loves us all,
The poor, the rich, the great, the small.
He is a friend who is always there
To share our troubles and lessen our care.
For no one is a stranger in God's sight,
For God is love, and in His light
May we, too, try in our small way
To make new friends from day to day.
So pass no stranger with an unseeing eye,
For God may be sending a new friend by.

~HSR

Sharing the Love of God

"I was hungry and you gave me something to eat,
I was thirsty and you gave me something to drink,
I was a stranger and you invited me in."

MATTHEW 25:35 NIV

There are more people living on our planet than ever before. We live close and work closer, yet loneliness and the absence of human connection plague us in epidemic proportions. Why are we more prone to pull inside our protective shells than to pursue a friendship with a stranger?

The Bible teaches that once we were all strangers to God, but He brought us close through His Son. It cost God dearly to reach out and make us His children, to call us brothers and friends. Following His example will require effort, even sacrifice, in extending ourselves to those who need to know someone cares. If we as the beneficiaries of God's love don't do it, who will?

Call a cheery hello to the neighbor across the fence. Take cookies and a word of welcome to the new family on the block. Be the first to greet visitors at your church. Addressing the supermarket cashier by name or extending a smile and helping hand to the harried mother in the post office can mean more than you will ever know. Whether your kindness is appreciated or rejected is beside the point. Do it even if it's difficult. Your efforts will bring joy to you and glory to your heavenly Father.

THE GIFT *of* FRIENDSHIP

Friendship is a priceless gift that cannot be bought or sold
But its value is far greater than a mountain made of gold—
For gold is cold and lifeless, it can neither see nor hear,
And in the time of trouble it is powerless to cheer.
It has no ears to listen, no heart to understand,
It cannot bring you comfort or reach out a helping hand—
So when you ask God for a gift be thankful if He sends
Not diamonds, pearls, or riches,

    but the love of real true friends.

~HSR

More Precious Than Gold

A friend loves at all times.
PROVERBS 17:17 NIV

Throughout history, gold, silver, and precious gems have been deemed, in and of themselves, the very currency of entire civilizations. In our day, a dollar bill, without gold to back it up, is just a piece of worthless paper. Precious minerals are valuable because they are rare, difficult to obtain, and absolutely genuine.

So it is with friendship. Developing it takes years of shared experience, decades of learning to trust, miles and miles of life's roads traveled together. Like a diamond in the rough, true friendship often develops slowly and endures tremendous pressure before it develops those sparkling characteristics that make it so valuable.

While casual relationships are like common stones that litter the ground at our feet, easy to pick up and easy to toss away, a true friend is much harder to find, greater in value than gold or silver. The Bible teaches that true friendship is important. Jesus deemed friendship with us of such great worth that He laid down His life to accomplish it.

We who have this kind of friendship need to strengthen it in sacrifice and faithful, selfless effort toward those God has called us to love and trustingly give ourselves to. The genuine friendships that God creates will endure and are more precious than anything else on earth!

LIFE IS *a* GARDEN

Life is a garden, good friends are the flowers,
And times spent together life's happiest hours...
And friendship, like flowers, blooms ever more fair
When carefully tended by dear friends who care...
And life's lovely garden would be sweeter by far
If all who passed through it were as nice as you are.

~HSR

The Beauty of Friendship

Keep on loving each other as brothers.

HEBREWS 13:1 NIV

God loves a garden! After all, He created Eden for walking and talking with His first friends.

The gardens of life are made rich by the friendships that flourish there. They pop up like new flowers and bloom their beauty into our lives, enlarging and renewing with each passing year. Their shapes and colors and varieties are endless! Friendships, like flowers, need careful tending. They must be watered regularly by acts of sacrifice and kindness, fed by faithfulness and fellowship, trimmed by the prayer and praise we bestow on one another.

But as surely as the deep roots of understanding and the fragrant blossoms of love come on to reward us, weeds of distrust, betrayal, and disagreement will thrust ugly prickly heads through the soil, too. If they are not pulled up by the roots as soon as they arise, they will choke and cripple our strongest and most cherished relationships. Discord among friends is like acid rain.

Attend your garden well, for each friendship that blossoms is precious and life-giving. Pluck out noxious strife, bitterness, or jealousy. Walk with God down each pathway and ask Him to use you to bless, prosper, and protect each tender bloom growing there.

THE GOLDEN CHAIN *of* FRIENDSHIP

Friendship is a golden chain,
    the links are friends so dear,
And like a rare and precious jewel,
    it's treasured more each year.
It's clasped together firmly
    with a love that's deep and true,
And it's rich with happy memories
    and fond recollections, too.
Time can't destroy its beauty,
    for as long as memory lives,
Years can't erase the pleasure
    that the joy of friendship gives. . .
For friendship is a priceless gift
    that can't be bought or sold,
And to have an understanding friend
    is worth far more than gold. . .
And the golden chain of friendship
    is a strong and blessed tie
Binding kindred hearts together
    as the years go passing by.

~HSR

Treasures of the Heart

*Be kind to one another, tender-hearted, forgiving
each other, just as God in Christ also has forgiven you.*

EPHESIANS 4:32 NASB

Fine jewelry must be cared for and protected. Would you leave a beautiful strand of pearls on the ground to be trampled, tangled, scratched, or broken? Never! You store them in protective silk, keep them clean and polished, have them mended when they break. You wear them with pride, knowing that an investment in their beauty enhances your own.

Friends are like fine jewels. Handled with care they reward our investment with increasing value as the years go by. Unfortunately, now and then they take a beating in life's daily grind, become damaged from misuse or carelessness. Fixing them is costly and may require you to be without them while the Master Jeweler makes crucial repairs. Perhaps they've just begun to show signs of fading and need time and attention to burnish them again to a high luster.

Can you imagine assigning a dollar value to that person you call your best friend? It would be impossible! The shared joys and struggles, the mutual understanding and trust that have grown up between you are beyond counting. If a precious friendship has somehow become abused or neglected, take care to mend it now! It is a gift from God and a treasure far above diamonds and pearls!

FRIENDS ARE LIFE'S GIFT *of* LOVE

If people like me didn't know people like you,
Life would lose its meaning and its richness, too. . .
For the friends that we make are life's gift of love,
And I think friends are sent right from heaven above. . .
And thinking of you somehow makes me feel
That God is love and He's very real.

~HSR

Friends—Who Needs Them?

The sweetness of a man's friend gives delight by hearty counsel.
PROVERBS 27:9 NKJV

A room full of people can be a lonely place. You may feel like there are invisible walls that separate you from everyone else. Then you see a friend's face or hear her voice and everything changes. We need friends.

Even Jesus made friends, and He spent time getting to know them. He ate meals with them, walked, talked, and worked with them. He shared His thoughts, ideas, and beliefs with them and shared in their griefs and joys.

In an age when Internet acquaintances are the norm, there may be people we call friends, yet barely know and have never met in person. There's nothing wrong with these relationships, but we must admit they do not go below the surface. We each need at least one true friend who really knows us and loves us for who we really are.

A friend may not always come wrapped in the package you are expecting. Your friend may not be much like you. She may look different than you imagined. She may have a different background and family situation than you do. God often chooses friends for us who encourage and strengthen us and who can influence us to make good choices. These people need us, too. Friendship is a two-way street.

Who needs friends? We all do. They are treasures worth finding and keeping.

GIVE US DAILY AWARENESS

On life's busy thoroughfares
We meet with angels unaware
So Father, make us kind and wise
So we may always recognize
The blessings that are ours to take,
The friendships that are ours to make
If we but open our heart's door wide
To let the sunshine of love inside
For God is not in far distant places
But in loving hearts and friendly faces.

~HSR

Finding a Friend

Be devoted to one another in brotherly love.
Honor one another above yourselves.

ROMANS 12:10 NIV

In L. M. Montgomery's story, *Anne of Green Gables*, Marilla said she had no time for imagination, and Anne replied, "How much you miss!" We do miss much. We are often in a rush, hurrying about our errands and work. We don't take time for details or to build friendships.

What if you took a day to notice the people you encounter and consider what sort of person each is and what kind of friend he or she might be? What sort of friend might you be to each person if you were to step up and reach out with a warm smile or a friendly wave?

Speaking first, introducing yourself to a newcomer, inviting an acquaintance into your home to share a cup of tea or a meal—all these are ways to find friends right where you are. It may take courage, but one new friendship gained is worth the trouble.

Think of the friendships you might have missed by choosing to hurry by people and never speak. At school, at church, in the grocery store. . .there are great people you haven't met. At work, in our neighborhoods. . .there are men, women, and children who need to know you. And it may be that you need to know them, too!

GOD'S MESSENGERS

The unexpected kindness from an unexpected place,
A hand outstretched in friendship,
    a smile on someone's face,
A word of understanding spoken in a time of trial
Are unexpected miracles that make life more worthwhile.
We know not how it happened that in an hour of need
Somebody out of nowhere proved to be a friend indeed. . .
For God has many messengers we fail to recognize,
But He sends them when we need them,
    and His ways are wondrous and wise. . .
So keep looking for an angel and keep listening to hear,
For on life's busy, crowded streets,
    you will find God's presence near.

~HSR

Winning Friends

Behold, how good and how pleasant it is
for brethren to dwell together in unity!

PSALM 133:1 NKJV

When a checker in the grocery store smiles and speaks to you in a kind voice it helps, doesn't it? You know what a difference a friendly face can make in any situation.

Even a stranger can be like a messenger from God when he steps close in a time of crisis. If you've ever had an accident, a car breakdown, or been critically ill or injured, and someone came to assist you or just sit with you, you know what a comfort it can be. Have you passed on the blessing by reaching out to comfort someone else?

Whom could you befriend? Whom do you see who might need a listening ear or a helping hand? Someone with a physical need may benefit from your help. Someone with a spiritual need may find the help he needs when he hears your words of wisdom. Someone with an emotional need may find answers that help him stabilize with your encouragement.

Little things like a pat on the back, a cup of coffee, or a bit of hospitality may be the turning point in a person's life journey.

Reach out and begin treating others the way you'd like to be treated. It's a proven way to win friends, and a friend's heart is indeed a prize worth winning.

A Friend Is *a* Gift *from* God

Among the great and glorious gifts our heavenly Father sends
Is the gift of understanding that we find in loving friends. . .
For somehow in the generous heart of loving,
      faithful friends,
The good God in His charity and wisdom always sends
A sense of understanding and the power of perception
And mixes these fine qualities with kindness and affection. . .
So when we need some sympathy or a friendly hand to touch
Or one who listens and speaks words that mean so much,
We seek a true and trusted friend in the knowledge
      that we'll find
A heart that's sympathetic and an understanding mind. . .
And often just without a word there seems to be a union
Of thoughts and kindred feelings, for God gives
      true friends communion.

~HSR

Being the Friend You Seek

A man that hath friends must shew himself friendly.

PROVERBS 18:24 KJV

D o you remember the first friend you ever made? It was a glorious feeling, wasn't it? That first connection with someone outside your family, someone your age, someone who liked you "just because." That special relationship provided a needed sense of affirmation and the assurance of an accepting world beyond the safety of immediate family.

It's possible, though, that as you grew older, you found it more difficult to make friends. Perhaps you developed shyness or some hurt or rejection left you unable to reach out to others. If so, ask God to heal and embolden you. Then just relax. The Bible says that the best way to win friends is to practice being a friend. So imagine what you would appreciate in a friend and give that to those you meet. Look for opportunities to be kind, generous, and understanding. Take time to listen and let your words be gentle and wise.

When you exhibit the qualities of a true friend, you will no longer want for friendship. Those who value kindness, generosity, understanding, and wisdom will be drawn to you, for these are the same qualities God uses to draw us into friendship with Himself.

Friends are gifts from God. They are worthy of your commitment and effort. Make many and treasure them with all your heart.

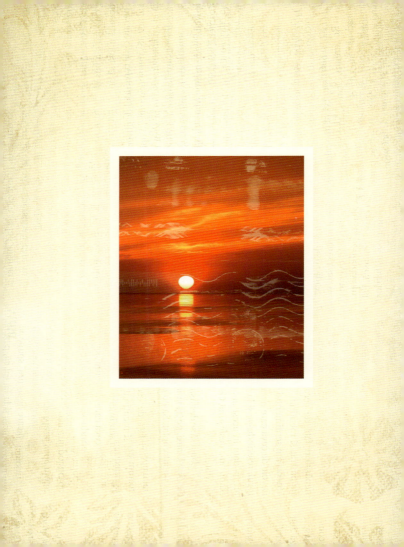

Widen My Vision

God, open my eyes so I may see
And feel Your presence close to me.
Give me strength for my stumbling feet
As I battle the crowd on life's busy street,
And widen the vision of my unseeing eyes
So in passing faces I'll recognize
Not just a stranger, unloved and unknown,
But a friend with a heart that is much like my own.
Give me perception to make me aware
That scattered profusely on life's thoroughfare
Are the best gifts of God that we daily pass by
As we look at the world with an unseeing eye.

~HSR

Heart's Eyes

"Blessed are your eyes, because they see;
and your ears, because they hear."

MATTHEW 13:16 NASB

Inside a popular mall, shoppers rush along the corridors, and teenagers amble in groups past the shops and cafés. Busy housewives, mothers with children in tow, and businessmen in their smart suits move steadily along, in and out of the stores and shops. A quiet woman sits on a park bench watching the action.

You've probably been there once or twice watching and listening to snippets of passing conversations, wondering about the lives of the people you see. But have you ever wondered what those same people think when they watch you? Would they see a friendly, open person with a smile of greeting?

A smile and a word of greeting, even a tip of a gentleman's hat were once the norm in a slower day and age. Now folks rush and hurry everywhere. Passing each other in the busy mall concourses, few people even make eye contact.

Just because that's how it is doesn't mean that's how it has to stay. Why not start a trend to bring back friendliness and social grace? Slow down your pace. Greet those you meet with a smile. Look at those you encounter with the eyes of your heart. The best treasures are friends you find along the roads of life. Don't miss out.

Heart Gifts

It's not the things that can be bought
That are life's richest treasures,
It's just the little gifts from the heart
That money cannot measure.
A cheerful smile, a friendly word,
A sympathetic nod,
Are priceless little treasures
From the storehouse of our God.
They are the things that can't be bought
With silver or with gold,
For thoughtfulness and kindness
And love are never sold.
They are the priceless things in life
For which no one can pay,
And the giver finds rich recompense
In giving them away.

~HSR

Generous Hearts

The way of the good person is like the light of dawn,
growing brighter and brighter until full daylight.

PROVERBS 4:18 NCV

During the coldest weather, homeless people take refuge in the city library and line up for a warm supper in the soup kitchen and a cot and blanket at the local mission. The town's citizens show they care by providing hats, warm socks, gloves, and coats. Thank God, there are always kind folks who care.

You have probably given to strangers, too. When you have, didn't you find yourself rewarded by God who cares about the poor and needy? By God who gave to all of us when we were needy and strangers.

Yet, material things are not all people need. Sometimes a weary soul needs a kind word, an encouraging response, or a helping hand. Every day someone will cross your path who needs you. A thoughtful gesture—something as seemingly unimportant as a handshake or a friendly smile.

Touching a life breaks down a barrier and changes you from stranger to friend. It opens doors into lives and gives you an opportunity to show the love of God. Showing of kindnesses can be more effective in reaching lost souls than the best preaching. What can you do today with the resources you have to help the needy and bless those less fortunate than yourself?

IT'S *a* WONDERFUL WORLD

In spite of the fact we complain and lament
And view this old world with much discontent,
Deploring conditions and grumbling because
There's so much injustice and so many flaws,
It's a wonderful world, and it's people like you
Who make it that way by the things that they do.
For a warm, ready smile or a kind, thoughtful deed
Or a hand outstretched in an hour of need
Can change our whole outlook and make the world bright
Where a minute before just nothing seemed right.
It's a wonderful world and it always will be
If we keep our eyes open and focused to see
The wonderful things we are capable of
When we open our hearts to God and His love.

~HSR

Being There for Others

We are God's workmanship, created in Christ Jesus to do good works, which God prepared in advance for us to do.

EPHESIANS 2:10 NIV

Maybe you've noticed that in times of great distress and disaster—terrorist attacks, earthquakes, tsunamis, or hurricanes, for example—something extraordinary happens. We all become friends. Acts of kindness even coupled with great danger and sacrifice are almost commonplace.

You've seen it. Groups of people abandon their lives for weeks to dig survivors from the rubble or provide much-needed medical care. Others travel long distances at their own expense to do whatever they can in the recovery effort. Nation reaches out to nation in those precarious times, but even more impressive is how people reach out to each other in truly sacrificial ways.

We live in a world that is guarded and unpredictable, but this tendency to come to the aid of others shows that God

has placed within each human being a sense of connectedness to others in the human family. That connectedness ex-
ists in the face of tragedy but also in ordinary times between
ordinary people. You don't need a disaster to be a friend to
those around you.

With wisdom always at the forefront, put yourself out there
for someone who is hurting or suffering lack. Get involved, and
pray about what you can do to help. True friendship is giving
to someone with no thought of receiving something in return.

Celebrating a
Mother's Love

MOTHERHOOD

The dearest gifts that heaven holds,
    the very finest, too,
Were made into one pattern
    that was perfect, sweet, and true.
The angels smiled, well pleased, and said,
    "Compared to all the others,
This pattern is so wonderful let's use it
    just for mothers!"
And through the years, a mother has been all
    that's sweet and good,
For there's a bit of God and love
    in all true motherhood.

~HSR

A Very Special Design

"Honor your father and mother, that your days may be prolonged in the land which the LORD your God gives you."

EXODUS 20:12 NASB

When God created Eve to be a helper and companion for Adam, He also made her the first mother of mankind. She, like all mothers since, was designed to conceive and nurture a child in the womb for nine long and crucial months. It is through that gestation process that an almost mystical bond is formed between mother and baby. If you are a mother, you can surely identify with this privilege.

We all—every one of us—need a mother. Beyond the physical processes of giving birth, God's perfect design for woman includes that empathy, closeness, understanding, and love that mothers share with their children. As strong as that bond is, however, it can be neglected, injured, or even destroyed. No doubt you've read statistics or observed firsthand the mental and emotional problems that can arise in children cut off from their mothers.

You are no doubt the child of a mother; and if you are a woman, chances are good that you are a mother as well. Make every effort to nurture those special relationships. Reach out today to reinforce or repair them if needed. It might take a simple phone call to say "I love you," or "Let's talk about it," that restores that wonderful bond and ushers in healing. Don't delay—do it today!

It Takes *a* Mother

It takes a mother's love to make a house a home—
A place to be remembered no matter where we roam.
It takes a mother's patience to bring a child up right
And her courage and her cheerfulness to make
    a dark day bright.
It takes a mother's thoughtfulness to mend
    the heart's deep hurts
And her skill and her endurance to mend little
    socks and shirts.
It takes a mother's kindness to forgive us when we err,
To sympathize in trouble and to bow her head in prayer.
It takes a mother's wisdom to recognize our needs
And to give us reassurance by her loving words and deeds.

~HSR

Motherhood's High Calling

Her children arise and call her blessed.

PROVERBS 31:28 NIV

A home is not made of four walls and a roof. It takes a very special touch to turn a mere house into a home. And for most of us that transformation was due to our mothers' diligent influence.

Despite how our culture would downplay the importance of the role of mothering, her job, when done well, is an amazing and essential one. Try to imagine the home you grew up in without your mother there. A well-run home is an institution in which mother is secretary, housekeeper, seamstress, laundress, chef, and chauffeur—all important roles, but minor in comparison to her higher calling as confidant, confessor, mediator, and judge. She soothes, cheerleads, doctors, and juggles schedules like a circus performer. She is a gifted listener and trusted prayer partner. Often, her few "free" moments are interrupted and her sleep troubled. And these are roles that must mingle with those of wife and helpmeet. "Full-time" does not even begin to describe her calling!

Is it any wonder that we set aside a day in honor of mothers each year? Surely, she deserves more than one! Our mothers are treasure beyond rubies, pearls of great price, and they are doing the most important job in the world. May we never be remiss in telling them so!

Mother Is *a* Word Called Love

Mother is a word called love,
And all the world is mindful of
That the love that's given and shown to others
Is different from the love of mothers. . .
No other love than mother love
Could do the things required of
The one whom God gives the keeping
Of His wee lambs, awake or sleeping. . .
So mothers are a special race
God sent to earth to take His place,
And "Mother" is a lovely name
That even saints are proud to claim.

~HSR

The Blessing of a Godly Mother

Train up a child in the way he should go,
and when he is old he will not depart from it.

PROVERBS 22:6 NKJV

It has been wisely observed that mothering is the hardest job in the world. It is a work in which joy and sorrow, failure and fulfillment, mingle in one huge role crucial to making each of us what we are today.

Like our heavenly Father, a good mother keeps her children close, protecting them from danger and injury. She nurtures and instructs, disciplining and correcting with gentle understanding and grace. She grieves when we fail and rejoices when we achieve. She hopes for us, believes in us, and is a fountain of mercy when we've gone wrong, a vital channel through which our Lord encourages and molds us. She is always demonstrating with love and forgiveness the pardon for sin God promises His repentant children.

If you are a mother, never let anyone disparage your high calling or tell you there are more important things to do.

Raising children to love and obey God, to respect themselves and others, to be gracious, generous, honest, and kind is a constant and demanding task requiring the most specialized of skills.

True mothering may be the hardest job in the world, but it is also a divine privilege and, as every good mother knows, the rewards, for herself and for her children, are beyond measure.

MOTHERS ARE
SPECIAL PEOPLE

Mothers are special people
In a million different ways,
And merit loving compliments
And many words of praise,
For a mother's aspiration
Is for her family's success,
To make the family proud of her
And bring them happiness. . .
And like our heavenly Father,
She's a patient, loving guide,
Someone we can count on
To be always on our side.

~HSR

He Gently Leads

He takes care of his people like a shepherd.
He gathers them like lambs in his arms and carries them
close to him. He gently leads the mothers of the lambs.

ISAIAH 40:11 NCV

Tucked high in the branches of the oak tree are the remains of a nest. The young birds have long since flown, and the winter wind that took the leaves from the oak has battered the nest once tightly bound together of rootlets and twigs. The mother bird sits at the feeder. She will rebuild the nest in the spring or start a new one and raise a new brood.

As a human mother you will find motherhood a longer lasting chore—one of eternal consequence. Giving birth is possibly the easiest part of the mothering journey, despite its reputation. Protecting, nurturing, feeding, and caring for a child is a difficult job. Teaching and training, disciplining and guiding the child through his growing years, and then gently sending him out to fly is an almost incomprehensible task. Only with God's help can you succeed in this very demanding role.

Lean on Jesus, who like a mother Himself, has loved you. He has set the example for you and acts as your tutor to help you to be the mom He created you to be. When the schedules and demands seem overwhelming, Jesus knows what to do. Let Him lead you as you mother the precious children He has given you.

A Mother's Love

A mother's love is something that no one can explain—
It is made of deep devotion and of sacrifice and pain.
It is endless and unselfish and enduring, come what may,
For nothing can destroy it or take that love away.
It is patient and forgiving when all others are forsaking,
And it never fails or falters even though
      the heart is breaking.
It believes beyond believing when the world
      around condemns,
And it glows with all the beauty of the rarest,
      brightest gems.
It is far beyond defining, it defies all explanation,
And it still remains a secret like the mysteries of creation—
A many-splendored miracle man cannot understand
And another wondrous evidence of God's tender,
      guiding hand.

~HSR

Such We Are

See how great a love the Father has bestowed on us,
that we would be called children of God, and such we are.

1 JOHN 3:1 NASB

It's a song known round the world, a song that seems to have a mysterious power to touch hearts: "Jesus loves me, this I know." You probably sang it when you were little and have sung it to your children. If only we, as mothers, could love our children as Jesus has loved us—with such simplicity and strength.

If you want your children to know the redeeming power of God's love, you will want to care for them as the Lord has for you. It can be difficult to do. Yet, since we love them so much, we find grace to bear with them though they have flaws. We can overlook all sorts of infractions and foibles because love is so strong.

God has called us His children, and He has forgiven us our many sins and remembered our human frailties. He has also disciplined us in the same way we must discipline our children when we truly care about them.

You love your children with an unreasonable love, despite the quarrels, messes, crying, and fussing. You love them and want to mother them as well as you can. God stands ready to lead you in this blessed chore. He, our parent, teaches us to be parents who can love as He loved.

A Mother's Day Prayer

Our Father in heaven, whose love is divine,
Thanks for the love of a mother like mine.
In Thy great mercy look down from above
And grant this dear mother the gift of Your love,
And all through the year, whatever betide her,
Assure her each day that You are beside her. . .
And, Father in heaven, show me the way
To lighten her tasks and brighten her day,
And bless her dear heart with the insight to see
That her love means more than the world to me.

~HSR

God's Promise to Mothers

The LORD is my strength and my shield;
my heart trusts in him, and I am helped.
My heart leaps for joy and
I will give thanks to him in song.

PSALM 28:7 NIV

Being a mother has never been easy. Even Eve, the very first mother, suffered the loss of one child at the hand of the other. It's certainly not a job for the faint of heart. And yet, God has placed in mothers a ferocity, a determination, and a penchant for sacrificial, unconditional love that transcends earthly understanding.

Playwright, author, and psychologist Florida Scott-Maxwell once said, "No matter how old a mother is, she watches her middle-aged children for signs of improvement." How true. A mother never retires. Though her job description changes, she continues to love, encourage, and pray for her children as long as she has breath to do so. Her fiery, protective heart never leaves her.

If you are a mother, you know the intense joy a child brings but also the days when your heart aches and emotion and stress seem to be swallowing you up. That's when you must understand that along with God's endowment of motherhood, He also gives you special access to His throne room. He has promised to partner with you, marshalling His mighty resources on behalf of your child. Open your heart to Him and He will help you be the mother He has called you to be—through the joy and the tears.

Celebrating

God's Love

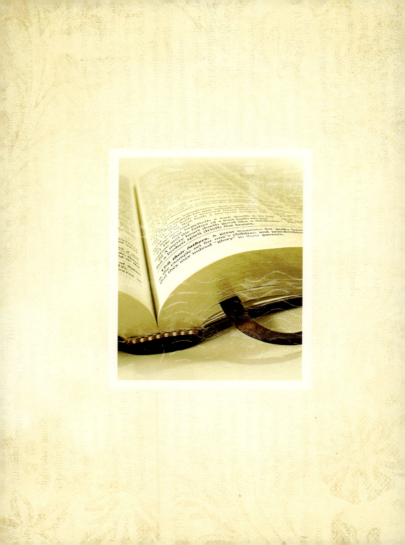

God's Love Is *a* Haven
in the Storms *of* Life

God's love is like an island in life's ocean vast and wide,
A peaceful, quiet shelter from the restless, rising tide.
God's love is like a fortress, and we seek protection there
When the waves of tribulation seem
      to drown us in despair.
God's love is a sanctuary where our souls can find
      sweet rest
From the struggle and the tension of life's fast
      and futile quest.
God's love is like a tower rising far above the crowd,
And God's smile is like the sunshine breaking
      through the threatening cloud.
God's love is like a beacon burning bright
      with faith and prayer,
And through all the changing scenes of life we can find
      a haven there.

~HSR

Calm in the Storm

For You are my rock and my fortress;
for Your name's sake You will lead me and guide me.

PSALM 31:3 NASB

During His years of ministry here on earth, Jesus' disciples became His closest friends. He had hand-picked each one, teaching them about His Father, His Kingdom, and His Purpose. He regularly rowed out with them on the Sea of Galilee for an evening of fishing and fellowship. These men loved Jesus and were beginning to trust Him as Lord of their lives.

Yet when a violent storm arose on the lake and threatened to swamp the boat, they panicked, fearing loss of life and livelihood. With a word, Jesus rebuked the wind and waves, and the storm subsided! Then, turning to His amazed disciples, He asked, "Where is your faith?"

Are there storms whipping your placid sea into towering waves that threaten to overcome and sink you? So often it's easy to trust Jesus when the skies are clear and the weather fine; but how quickly we are tempted to surrender to fear and doubt when our sea grows restless!

Remember, the same God who calmed the Sea of Galilee can quell any storm that rocks your little boat. He is the same Lord to whom even the winds of adversity and waves of affliction must submit when he says, "Peace. . .be still."

Somebody Cares

Somebody cares and always will,
The world forgets, but God loves you still
You cannot go beyond His love
No matter what you're guilty of,
For God forgives until the end,
He is your faithful, loyal friend. . . .

~HSR

A True Friend

There is a friend who sticks closer than a brother.

PROVERBS 18:24 NIV

Who are your friends? Are they folks with whom you work or attend church? Perhaps they live next door, occasionally borrow an egg or a cup of sugar, agree to water your plants when you travel. Maybe you cheer one another's children at soccer games on Saturday mornings, exchange cookies at Christmas, and swap "How are you?" in the grocery store.

We're all drawn to these pleasant relationships that don't require a great deal of commitment, risk, or sacrifice. They fit us like a light sweater on a fair day.

But who is there for us when life stirs up a genuine storm? When we're experiencing deep physical or emotional pain? When the guilt of a sinful act bears down to the breaking point? These are the times when we need a true friend.

God loves us despite how filthy, battered, or unlovely we become. He's aware of our private agonies, secret sins, and wrong motives. When earthly friends turn to flee, He moves closer. He's the one who comes to find us hiding in the hole we've dug for ourselves, pulls us out, and cleans us up, applies the bandages, and rejoices over us as we heal.

His love is unconditional and powerful, His grace boundless, and His faithfulness unflagging. Trust Him, depend on Him. . .call Him "friend."

THIS TOO WILL PASS AWAY

If I can endure for this minute
      whatever is happening to me
No matter how heavy my heart is
      or how dark the moment might be—
If I can remain calm and quiet
      with all my world crashing about me,
Secure in the knowledge God loves me
      when everyone else seems to doubt me—
If I can but keep on believing what
      I know in my heart to be true,
That darkness will fade with the morning
      and that this will pass away, too—
Then nothing in life can defeat me,
      for as long as this knowledge remains,
I can suffer whatever is happening,
      for I know God will break all the chains
That are binding me tight in the darkness
      and trying to fill me with fear. . .
For there is no night without dawning,
      and I know that my morning is near.

~HSR

Waiting for the Dawn

"Fear not, for I am with you; be not dismayed,
for I am your God. I will strengthen you, yes, I will help you,
I will uphold you with My righteous right hand."

Isaiah 41:10 NKJV

Dear one, if you have not yet experienced the dark night of the soul, brace yourself—sooner or later it comes to us all!

This is no ordinary hardship, but trouble that wants to tear your heart out: life-threatening illness, a marriage on the rocks, job loss, or a paycheck that simply will not stretch to meet your basic needs, a rebellious child or unjust accusation that could ruin a reputation or destroy a friendship.

King David, before he came to his throne, spent many a lonely night hiding from Saul in dark caves of despair, pouring out his sorrowing heart to God. Even our Savior, in Gethsemane, on the night of His betrayal, pled with His Father to "let this cup pass from Me." Because He overcame, so shall we!

When the agony of suffering envelops you, remember, the same power that rescued David and enabled Jesus to rise and fulfill God's plan is yours as well. Cling to Christ's example: humility and trust in our heavenly Father's love and care. As surely as there is a dark night of the soul, there will come the glorious dawn of God's protection, comfort, and deliverance. And if He is for us, who—or what—can be against us!

"Love Divine,
All Loves Excelling"

In a myriad of miraculous ways
God shapes our lives and changes our days.
Beyond our will or even knowing
God keeps our spirits ever growing. . .
For lights and shadows, sun and rain,
Sadness and gladness, joy and pain
Combine to make our lives complete
And give us victory through defeat.
Oh "Love divine, all loves excelling,"
In troubled hearts You just keep on dwelling,
Patiently waiting for a prodigal son
To say at last, "Thy will be done."

~HSR

A Love for All

This is what real love is: It is not our love for God; it is God's love for us. He sent his Son to die in our place to take away our sins.

1 JOHN 4:10 NCV

In the chapel of the children's hospital, a father kneels praying for his sick child. He prays that the cancer will not take his child's breath, that his little girl would wake and smile and play. He begs God's mercy, and then he wipes his tears and goes back down the hall to the child's bedside. It's a drama so sad that it is almost unbearable, but it has happened many times—a parent grieves while he watches his child die. If it were possible, he would die in the child's place—if only.

Maybe you've known someone who was suffering so, and you felt helpless to bring comfort to the situation. Know that when you can't, God can. God understands for He faced losing us to sin and the devil. He was so determined to rescue us that He gave the life of His only Son for us.

God can comfort hearts when you can't. He knows how to bring the comfort necessary for such extreme grief and heartache. His love is strong and consistent. When we are weakest, He is strongest.

You as God's representative on the earth can offer words of comfort and a caring shoulder to lean on. You can point to the true help in such overwhelming situations—the Lord our God.

HE LOVES YOU

It's amazing and incredible, but it's as true as it can be,
God loves and understands us all,
    and that means you and me.
He grace is all-sufficient for both the young and old,
For the lonely and the timid, for the brash and for the bold.
His love knows no exceptions, so never feel excluded,
No matter who or what you are,
    your name has been included. . .
And no matter what your past has been,
    trust God to understand,
And no matter what your problem is,
    just place it in His hand. . .
For in all our unloveliness this great God loves us still,
He loved us since the world began,
    and what's more, He always will!

~HSR

Lover of Young and Old

"I have carried you since you were born;
I have taken care of you from your birth.
Even when you are old, I will be the same.
Even when your hair has turned gray,
I will take care of you."

ISAIAH 46:3–4 NCV

A cheery voice was heard in the hospital room. "How are you doing today, sweetheart?" What a change came over the old woman's face! The atmosphere of the room instantly changed from dreary and sterile to personal and warm. It is amazing to see how a gesture of kindness can make a big difference in the day for a sick or elderly person.

It's comforting to family, too, to see their relative treated well. We dread growing old ourselves and fear we will be neglected or mistreated. God promises to be with us when we are old and to take care of us. Isn't that a comfort to consider—God with us offering us the comfort of His company and assistance?

Even when you are old and need care. . .when you can no longer serve your family or community, God will be with you. When your hair turns gray and your arms too weak to lift another, your legs too weak to go places for Him, He will treat you as He has always treated you—with loving-kindness and faithfulness.

Knowing that should make us kinder, more patient and considerate, more careful to remember others, to be gentler to all we encounter. To smile and give attention to the lonely and the disheartened is Christlike and a blessing bestowed.

What More Can You Ask?

God's love endures forever,
    what a wonderful thing to know
When the tides of life run against you
    and your spirit is downcast and low.
God's kindness is ever around you
    always ready to freely impart
Strength to your faltering spirit,
    cheer to your lonely heart.
God's presence is ever beside you,
    as near as the reach of your hand.
You have but to tell Him your troubles,
    there is nothing He won't understand. . .
And knowing God's love is unfailing,
    and His mercy unending and great,
You have but to trust in His promise,
    "God comes not too soon or too late". . .
So wait with a heart that is patient
    for the goodness of God to prevail,
For never do prayers go unanswered,
    and His mercy and love never fail.

~HSR

Heavenly Father,

You are the source of love, the initiator, and the inspiration. Wherever love can be seen, it is a reflection of Your person, character, and presence. Help us to step back from the busyness of our daily lives and celebrate the love You have so generously given us.

Amen.

Born in 1900 in Ohio, Helen Steiner Rice began writing at an early age. In 1918, Helen took a job at a public utilities company, eventually becoming one of the first female advertising managers and public speakers in the country. At age twenty-nine, she married banker Franklin Rice, who committed suicide in 1932, never having recovered mentally and financially from losses incurred during the Great Depression.

Following her husband's death, Helen used her gift of verse to encourage others. Her talents came to the attention of the nation when her greeting card poem "The Priceless Gift of Christmas" was read on *The Lawrence Welk Show*. Soon a series of poetry books, a source of inspiration to people worldwide, followed. Helen died in 1981, leaving a foundation that offers assistance to the needy and elderly.

Scripture Index

NOTES